HE CONSTITUTION EXPLAINED!

ARTICLE III

UILDING THE COURT SYSTEM

BY FLETCHER C. FINCH

Gareth Stevens PUBLISHING

Please visit our website, www.garethstevens.com. For a free color catalog of all our high-quality books, call toll free 1-800-542-2595 or fax 1-877-542-2596.

Library of Congress Cataloging-in-Publication Data

Names: Finch, Fletcher C.
Title: Article III: building the court system / Fletcher C. Finch.
Description: New York : Gareth Stevens Publishing, 2021. | Series: The Constitution explained! | Includes glossary and index.
Identifiers: ISBN 9781538258583 (pbk.) | ISBN 9781538258606 (library bound) | ISBN 9781538258590 (6 pack)
Subjects: LCSH: Courts–United States–Juvenile literature. | United States. Constitution. Article 3.
Classification: LCC KF8720.F56 2021 | DDC 347.73'2–dc23

First Edition

Published in 2021 by
Gareth Stevens Publishing
111 East 14th Street, Suite 349
New York, NY 10003

Designer: Sarah Liddell
Editor: Therese Shea

Photo credits: Cover, (main) Cameron Whitman/Shutterstock.com; background texture used throughout Lukasz Szwaj/Shutterstock.com; p. 5 Drew Angerer/Staff/Getty Images News/Getty Images; p. 7 Chip Somodevilla/Staff/Getty Images News/Getty Images; pp. 9, 21 Bloomberg/Contributor/Bloomberg/Getty Images; p. 11 Sergei Savostyanov/Contributor/TASS/Getty Images; p. 13 The Washington Post/Contributor/The Washington Post/Getty Images; pp. 15, 27 Bettmann/Contributor/Bettmann/Getty Images; p. 17 Ulrich Baumgarten/Contributor/Ulrich Baumgarten/Getty Images; p. 19 Francis Miller/Contributor/The LIFE Picture Collection/Getty Images; p. 23 Library of Congress/Contributor/Corbis Historical/Getty Images; p. 25 Kean Collection/Staff/Archive Photos/Getty Images; p. 29 Richard Sharrocks/Moment/Getty Images.

Printed in the United States of America

CPSIA compliance information: Batch #CS20GS: For further information contact Gareth Stevens, New York, New York at 1-800-542-2595.

CONTENTS

WORDS IN THE GLOSSARY APPEAR IN **BOLD** TYPE THE FIRST TIME THEY ARE USED IN THE TEXT.

THE THIRD BRANCH

The federal, or national, government of the United States consists of three branches. Simply put, the legislative branch—Congress—creates the laws for the nation. The executive branch, headed by the president, enforces and carries out the laws. The **judicial** branch, made up of the Supreme Court and other federal courts, interprets the laws. These courts decide how laws apply to certain cases. The Supreme Court, the highest court, also has the power to strike down laws that don't follow the U.S. Constitution.

The U.S. Constitution is the highest law in the nation. It states the duties, responsibilities, and limits of each branch of government. The judicial branch is discussed in the part of the Constitution labeled Article III. The Constitution's writers planned a powerful, fair, and independent court system.

UNITED STATES GOVERNMENT

LEGISLATIVE:
CONGRESS
(SENATE, HOUSE OF REPRESENTATIVES)
↓
PASSES LAWS

EXECUTIVE:
PRESIDENT
VICE PRESIDENT
CABINET MEMBERS
DEPARTMENTS AND AGENCIES
↓
CARRIES OUT LAWS

JUDICIAL:
SUPREME COURT
FEDERAL COURTS
↓
INTERPRETS LAWS

CHECKS AND BALANCES

Having three branches does more than organize the work of the government. This arrangement separates the powers of the government. Each branch has different areas it controls. Each branch also has ways to "check," or limit the power of the other branches. For example, the president leads the military, but Congress makes the decision whether to declare war. These checks help keep power balanced. It makes sure that one branch doesn't misuse its power too.

DECISIONS BY THE JUDICIAL BRANCH CAN AFFECT ALL AMERICANS. IN 2019, PEOPLE GATHERED IN FRONT OF THE SUPREME COURT BUILDING AS JUSTICES WERE CONSIDERING A CASE ABOUT A NEW YORK CITY GUN LAW.

A CLOSER LOOK

THE CONSTITUTION BUILDS ON EARLIER IDEAS. A BOOK PUBLISHED IN 1748 BY FRENCH THINKER MONTESQUIEU STATED THAT EXECUTIVE, LEGISLATIVE, AND JUDICIAL POWERS OF GOVERNMENT NEED TO BE SEPARATE TO PROTECT PEOPLE'S LIBERTY.

CREATING THE SUPREME COURT

Section 1 of Article III of the Constitution begins by calling for the creation of the Supreme Court, and other federal courts if needed: **"THE JUDICIAL POWER OF THE UNITED STATES, SHALL BE VESTED IN ONE SUPREME COURT, AND IN SUCH INFERIOR COURTS AS THE CONGRESS MAY FROM TIME TO TIME ORDAIN AND ESTABLISH."**

"JUDICIAL POWER" is the authority to make a decision in a legal case. When the Constitution says that power is **"VESTED IN"** the courts, it means the role of making those decisions is given to the federal courts.

The Supreme Court is the highest court. The **"INFERIOR COURTS"** are lower, not worse, than the Supreme Court. The Supreme Court can overturn, or reverse, lower court decisions. Congress received the power to set up lower federal courts from the Constitution.

A CLOSER LOOK

IN THE NEWS AND OTHER PLACES, THE NAME FOR THE SUPREME COURT OF THE UNITED STATES IS SOMETIMES ABBREVIATED, OR SHORTENED, TO INITIALS: SCOTUS.

CONGRESS GETS TO WORK

After the Constitution took effect, Congress passed the Federal Judiciary Act of 1789. The act stated the Supreme Court should have one chief justice and five associate justices. It also split the nation into districts. Each district had its own district court. Circuit courts were established to cover groups of districts. Circuit courts are above district courts, but below the Supreme Court. This three-level federal court system is still in place.

THE MEMBERS OF THE U.S. SUPREME COURT POSE TOGETHER IN 2018. SINCE 1869, THE NUMBER OF SUPREME COURT JUSTICES HAS BEEN SET AT NINE.

INDEPENDENT JUDGES

Courts need freedom to make fair decisions. The Constitution protects federal judges' independence. Article III Section 1 says, **"THE JUDGES, BOTH OF THE SUPREME AND INFERIOR COURTS, SHALL HOLD THEIR OFFICES DURING GOOD BEHAVIOUR, AND SHALL, AT STATED TIMES, RECEIVE FOR THEIR SERVICES, A COMPENSATION, WHICH SHALL NOT BE DIMINISHED DURING THEIR CONTINUANCE IN OFFICE."**

This means federal judges can stay in office for life. They can't be removed for unpopular decisions. If a judge does something seriously wrong, the House of Representatives can impeach the judge, which means charge them with misconduct. Then the Senate votes on whether the judge is guilty. Only then can a judge be removed.

Section 1 also says judges' compensation, or pay, can't be cut. So, they can't be punished or controlled through their pay.

A CLOSER LOOK

THE U.S. PRESIDENT HAS THE POWER TO NOMINATE FEDERAL JUDGES, ACCORDING TO ARTICLE II OF THE CONSTITUTION. THE SENATE DECIDES WHETHER TO APPROVE THE NOMINATION.

LEARNING FROM THE PAST

Before the American Revolution, Great Britain's king had a lot of power over British courts. The Declaration of Independence accuses George III of controlling judges' pay and time in office. The writers of the Constitution wanted to protect U.S. courts. Founding Father Alexander Hamilton called courts the weakest part of government. He worried that judges could be overpowered or influenced by other branches of government. Keeping judges in office for life would allow courts to be independent, Hamilton wrote.

RUTH BADER GINSBURG BECAME A SUPREME COURT JUSTICE IN 1993. JUDGES MAY STAY IN OFFICE FOR LIFE. SHE CHOSE TO REMAIN ON THE SUPREME COURT EVEN WHEN SHE WAS BEING TREATED FOR CANCER IN 1999, 2009, AND 2019.

FEDERAL CASES

Section 2 of Article III names the types of legal issues that federal courts can decide. This is known as the **jurisdiction** of the courts.

The list begins, **"THE JUDICIAL POWER SHALL EXTEND TO ALL CASES, IN LAW AND EQUITY, ARISING UNDER THIS CONSTITUTION, THE LAWS OF THE UNITED STATES, AND TREATIES MADE, OR WHICH SHALL BE MADE, UNDER THEIR AUTHORITY."** These words give federal courts the role of judging **lawsuits** related to national laws and matters.

Federal courts are given jurisdiction **"TO ALL CASES AFFECTING AMBASSADORS, OTHER PUBLIC MINISTERS AND CONSULS."** These are names for diplomats who represent one nation to another. Federal judicial power also reaches **"TO ALL CASES OF ADMIRALTY AND MARITIME JURISDICTION."** This means cases dealing with ships, oceans, and certain waterways.

A CLOSER LOOK

TREATIES ARE AGREEMENTS BETWEEN COUNTRIES. LIKE THE CONSTITUTION AND OTHER FEDERAL LAWS, THEY AFFECT THE UNITED STATES AS A NATION.

"ALL CASES, IN LAW AND EQUITY"

In the British legal tradition, there were two types of courts, courts of law and courts of equity. They had developed side by side over hundreds of years. Courts of law dealt with written laws and followed strict procedures. They decided how the law applied to a case. Courts of equity worked to correct unfair situations. Equity means fairness. These courts had more **flexibility** about how to correct injustice. U.S. federal courts cover both types of cases.

FEDERAL COURTS CONSIDER CASES WHEN NATIONAL LAWS ARE BROKEN. MARIA BUTINA CAME TO THE UNITED STATES FROM RUSSIA AS A STUDENT. IN 2018, SHE WAS ARRESTED AND CHARGED WITH SECRETLY ACTING AS AN AGENT OF THE RUSSIAN GOVERNMENT. A FEDERAL JUDGE SENTENCED HER TO 18 MONTHS IN PRISON.

LEGAL CONTROVERSIES

Article III Section 2 states that federal courts' jurisdiction depends on who is involved. Courts' power extends **"TO CONTROVERSIES TO WHICH THE UNITED STATES SHALL BE A PARTY;—TO CONTROVERSIES BETWEEN TWO OR MORE STATES;— BETWEEN A STATE AND CITIZENS OF ANOTHER STATE;—BETWEEN CITIZENS OF DIFFERENT STATES;—BETWEEN CITIZENS OF THE SAME STATE CLAIMING LANDS UNDER GRANTS OF DIFFERENT STATES, AND BETWEEN A STATE, OR THE CITIZENS THEREOF, AND FOREIGN STATES, CITIZENS OR SUBJECTS."**

A "party" is a person or organization affected by the decision in a lawsuit. If the U.S. government is a party, a federal court judges the issue. Federal courts act as a kind of **referee** when state governments argue too. Federal courts also hear disagreements that cross state or national borders.

A CLOSER LOOK

THE ARTICLES OF CONFEDERATION WAS THE BASIS FOR THE UNITED STATES GOVERNMENT BEFORE THE CONSTITUTION. IT DIDN'T INCLUDE A NATIONAL COURT SYSTEM, HOWEVER.

THE ELEVENTH AMENDMENT

The Constitution is the highest law in the nation, but it can be changed or added to through an amendment. The Eleventh Amendment limited the judicial power that had been set in Article III. The amendment says federal courts cannot judge lawsuits against states that are brought by citizens from another state or country. It also allows states some protection against certain suits by their own citizens. Congress and state governments approved the change to protect states' rights.

STATES HAVE DISAGREED WITH THE FEDERAL GOVERNMENT ON ISSUES RELATED TO **IMMIGRATION**. IN 2018, 17 STATES AND WASHINGTON, DC, SUED THE FEDERAL GOVERNMENT OVER THE SEPARATION OF MIGRANT CHILDREN AND THEIR PARENTS AFTER THEY CROSSED INTO THE COUNTRY ILLEGALLY.

LIMITS ON FEDERAL COURTS

The wording in the Constitution allows some powers but limits others. Article III gives federal courts power over the cases and controversies listed. Those are the only types of issues where the federal courts have power. Article III also limits the courts to judging actual court cases. In 1793, President George Washington wanted the Supreme Court's advice on the rules under a treaty with France. The court noted it would be improper to give advice.

Federal courts also cannot judge cases when it's too late for a decision to matter. For example, if the case is against a person who has died, it's too late for a decision and the case is considered "moot." Supreme Court justices also cannot create new cases. The court can only decide on cases brought to it.

A CLOSER LOOK

A PERSON OR ORGANIZATION BRINGING A LAWSUIT TO FEDERAL COURT NEEDS TO HAVE "STANDING" IN THE CASE. THAT MEANS THAT AN ACTION OR DISAGREEMENT HAS ACTUALLY CAUSED THEM HARM.

STUDENT EXPRESSION

In 1965, students Mary Beth and John Tinker and Christopher Eckhardt expressed their wish for the end of the Vietnam War by wearing black armbands. Their school in Des Moines, Iowa, suspended them. The Tinkers' parents brought a lawsuit against the school district, saying students had free speech rights under the First Amendment. The case rose to the Supreme Court which ruled students don't lose their rights at school and wearing armbands didn't stop students from learning.

STUDENTS MARY BETH AND JOHN TINKER WANTED TO WEAR ARMBANDS TO CALL FOR PEACE DURING THE VIETNAM WAR. THE SUPREME COURT'S DECISION IN THEIR CASE CHANGED THE UNDERSTANDING OF STUDENTS' RIGHTS.

ORIGINAL JURISDICTION

Nearly all cases the Supreme Court hears were first heard in lower federal courts. The Court's role is to review those courts' decisions. However, in some situations, **"AFFECTING AMBASSADORS, OTHER PUBLIC MINISTERS AND CONSULS, AND THOSE IN WHICH A STATE SHALL BE PARTY,"** the Supreme Court can be the first to hear the case. This is called **"ORIGINAL JURISDICTION"** in Article III Section 2. The court doesn't have to wait for the case to come up through lower courts.

Over the years, the Supreme Court hasn't heard many cases of this type. When it does, they're usually cases in which one state disagrees with another. These can be disputes over state borders or water rights. The Supreme Court also has original jurisdiction if the U.S. government files a lawsuit against a state.

A CLOSER LOOK

THE SUPREME COURT CAN DECIDE NOT TO HEAR A CASE EVEN WHEN IT HAS ORIGINAL JURISDICTION.

STATE VERSUS STATE

In 1998, the Supreme Court decided a case in which New York and New Jersey disagreed over the ownership of Ellis Island. An agreement in 1834 had given ownership of the island itself to New York and the water around it to New Jersey. Over the years, the island was expanded by dumping earth around its shoreline. The court decided that New York owned the original island and New Jersey owned the land that had been added.

ELLIS ISLAND WAS THE PLACE MANY IMMIGRANTS ENTERED THE UNITED STATES BETWEEN 1892 AND 1954. WHEN NEW YORK AND NEW JERSEY FOUGHT OVER OWNERSHIP OF THE ISLAND, THE CASE WENT TO THE SUPREME COURT.

HEARING APPEALS

So how does a case from a lower court reach the Supreme Court? If a person involved in that case thinks something is wrong with a court's judgment, they can try to **appeal** that decision. The person making the appeal asks a higher court to review the decision.

Article III Section 2 says, **"IN ALL THE OTHER CASES BEFORE MENTIONED, THE SUPREME COURT SHALL HAVE APPELLATE JURISDICTION, BOTH AS TO LAW AND FACT, WITH SUCH EXCEPTIONS, AND UNDER SUCH REGULATIONS AS THE CONGRESS SHALL MAKE."** The Supreme Court's power to review cases from lower courts is called appellate jurisdiction. Appellate means relating to an appeal.

In reviewing a case, justices consider the actions of the lower court, the laws applied in a decision, and the specifics of a case.

APPEALING TO THE SUPREME COURT

FEDERAL TRIAL COURT (DISTRICT) → U.S. APPEALS COURT (CIRCUIT) → U.S. SUPREME COURT

STATE TRIAL COURT → STATE APPEALS COURT → STATE SUPREME COURT → U.S. SUPREME COURT

A CONSTITUTIONAL QUESTION

In 1958, Mildred and Richard Loving were sentenced to prison. They had broken a Virginia law that banned white and black people from marrying each other. The Supreme Court heard their appeal since it related to the Constitution. The Fourteenth Amendment says all people have equal protection of the law. The Supreme Court said the Virginia marriage law treated people unequally, however. Since the law **violated** people's constitutional rights, the Court overturned it.

THE MARRIAGE OF RICHARD AND MILDRED LOVING BROKE A STATE LAW, BUT THE LAW WENT AGAINST THE PROTECTIONS OF THE U.S. CONSTITUTION.

A CLOSER LOOK

IF THE SUPREME COURT DECIDES NOT TO CONSIDER AN APPEAL, THE DECISION OF THE LOWER COURT STAYS IN EFFECT.

JUDICIAL REVIEW

Federal courts' ability to review and even overturn the laws created by Congress or a president's **executive orders** is called judicial review. The Constitution doesn't mention judicial review exactly. Scholars say the power is implied in two articles. Article III calls on the judicial branch to decide cases relating to the Constitution and U.S. laws. Article VI says that all **"JUDICIAL OFFICERS, BOTH OF THE UNITED STATES AND OF THE SEVERAL STATES, SHALL BE BOUND . . . TO SUPPORT THIS CONSTITUTION."**

Chief Justice John Marshall explained judicial review in the 1803 decision for the case *Marbury v. Madison*. Marshall said it is "the province and duty of the Judicial Department to say what the law is . . . If two laws conflict with each other, the Courts must decide on the operation of each."

A CLOSER LOOK

JUDGES HAVE DIFFERENT WAYS OF UNDERSTANDING THE CONSTITUTION AND APPROACHING COURT CASES. THE BELIEFS OF EACH SUPREME COURT JUSTICE CAN MAKE A BIG DIFFERENCE IN THEIR DECISIONS.

PACKING THE COURT

Presidents try to direct future judicial decisions through their nominations to the Supreme Court. The Senate can block or approve nominations, however. In the 1930s, the Supreme Court overturned several of President Franklin D. Roosevelt's laws. Roosevelt backed a bill to add justices. Congress thought Roosevelt was trying to "pack the court." If Roosevelt appointed more justices who agreed with him, future decisions might go his way. The bill was voted down.

LAWYER DANA NESSEL (LEFT) CELEBRATES WITH JAYNE ROWSE (CENTER) AND APRIL DEBOER (RIGHT) WHO SUED MICHIGAN OVER THE STATE'S BAN ON SAME-SEX MARRIAGE. IN A 2015 DECISION, THE SUPREME COURT SAID THAT LAWS AGAINST SAME-SEX MARRIAGE VIOLATED THE CONSTITUTION.

TRIAL BY JURY

The writers of the Constitution wanted to protect personal freedoms and prevent government misconduct. That's why citizens, not judges or government agents, make the decision in a jury trial.

Article III Section 2 says, **"THE TRIAL OF ALL CRIMES, EXCEPT IN CASES OF IMPEACHMENT, SHALL BE BY JURY; AND SUCH TRIAL SHALL BE HELD IN THE STATE WHERE THE SAID CRIMES SHALL HAVE BEEN COMMITTED; BUT WHEN NOT COMMITTED WITHIN ANY STATE, THE TRIAL SHALL BE AT SUCH PLACE OR PLACES AS THE CONGRESS MAY BY LAW HAVE DIRECTED."**

Members of a jury consider whether the government has enough proof against a person who has been accused of a crime. This can add a layer of protection against abuse. The impeachment process mentioned is set up in other parts of the Constitution.

A CLOSER LOOK

THE WRITERS OF THE CONSTITUTION THOUGHT IT WAS ONLY FAIR TO HAVE A TRIAL NEAR THE LOCATION WHERE AN OFFENSE IS SAID TO HAVE TAKEN PLACE. THIS WAS A REACTION TO UNFAIR PRACTICES COLONISTS EXPERIENCED UNDER BRITISH RULE.

THE TRIAL OF SUSAN B. ANTHONY

In 1872, Susan B. Anthony was arrested for voting, breaking both state and federal law. Anthony said she was a U.S. citizen and the Fourteenth Amendment allowed her to vote. In a federal trial, the judge said the Fourteenth Amendment didn't promise voting rights to women. He told the jury to find Anthony guilty. In an 1895 case, the Supreme Court said a court cannot tell jurors to find someone guilty. In 1920, the Nineteenth Amendment guaranteed women's right to vote.

THE CASE *UNITED STATES V. SUSAN B. ANTHONY* REVEALS THAT HAVING A JURY DOESN'T ALWAYS MEAN HAVING A FAIR TRIAL.

TREASON AGAINST THE UNITED STATES

Treason is when someone betrays their country. It's the only crime the Constitution defines: **"TREASON AGAINST THE UNITED STATES, SHALL CONSIST ONLY IN LEVYING [DECLARING] WAR AGAINST THEM, OR IN ADHERING TO [JOINING] THEIR ENEMIES, GIVING THEM AID AND COMFORT."**

Here, in Section 3 of Article III, the writers of the Constitution were responding to abuses colonists had experienced under British law. The Constitution makes it clear that only certain actions can be considered treason. Making war directly against the United States is treason, and so is taking action to help the nation's enemies.

Section 3 also sets rules for proving treason. It says, **"NO PERSON SHALL BE CONVICTED OF TREASON UNLESS ON THE TESTIMONY OF TWO WITNESSES TO THE SAME OVERT ACT, OR ON CONFESSION IN OPEN COURT."**

A CLOSER LOOK

IN LEGAL LANGUAGE, AN "OVERT ACT" IS A STEP TAKEN BY SOMEONE IN ORDER TO COMMIT A CRIME. THE ACTION MIGHT BE LEGAL ON ITS OWN, BUT IT'S PART OF AN ILLEGAL PLAN.

THE TRIAL OF AARON BURR

Aaron Burr, the former vice president, had gone west in 1805 and gathered a group of supporters. He was accused of trying to get people in western areas to break away from the United States. Burr was charged with treason. Chief Justice John Marshall judged the case. He said the jury needed to consider whether Burr had clearly taken part in an act of war against the United States. The jury found Burr not guilty.

AARON BURR'S TREASON TRIAL CAME AFTER AN EARLIER SCANDAL. WHILE BURR WAS VICE PRESIDENT, HE SHOT FORMER SECRETARY OF THE TREASURY ALEXANDER HAMILTON IN A **DUEL**.

PUNISHING TREASON

The punishment for treason is limited. This is also a reaction to British law. Article III ends by stating, **"THE CONGRESS SHALL HAVE POWER TO DECLARE THE PUNISHMENT OF TREASON, BUT NO ATTAINDER OF TREASON SHALL WORK CORRUPTION OF BLOOD, OR FORFEITURE EXCEPT DURING THE LIFE OF THE PERSON ATTAINTED."**

Under British law, a person who committed treason was **"ATTAINTED."** That means they lost certain rights, including the right to own and pass on property. **"CORRUPTION OF BLOOD"** meant an attainted person's family couldn't receive property from that person. Article III limits punishment to only the person guilty of treason.

Several treason cases came to the Supreme Court relating to World War II (1939–1945). The court stated treason must "consist of something outward and visible and capable of direct proof."

A CLOSER LOOK

IN LAW, FORFEITURE IS WHEN SOMEONE LOSES PROPERTY OR GIVES IT TO THE GOVERNMENT AS PUNISHMENT FOR A CRIME.

BRITISH ROOTS

The American legal system grew from Great Britain's system. The newly independent colonies kept many British traditions, changed some, and totally rejected others. Many legal phrases and processes stayed the same. Jury trials were a feature of British law, for example. However, the Constitution banned the British practice of "corruption of blood" for treason and "ex post facto" laws, which punish someone for an action that was legal at the time it was done.

TREASON IS A CRIME THAT SUPPORTS THE ENEMIES OF THE UNITED STATES DURING WARTIME. AMERICAN PILOT MARTIN MONTI, JR. WAS CONVICTED OF COMMITTING TREASON AGAINST THE UNITED STATES DURING WORLD WAR II.

AN ACTIVE INSTITUTION

Article III established judicial power. For more than 230 years, the judicial branch has helped shape the government and the nation itself. Federal courts have heard cases and judged laws on topics including slavery, borders, voting rights, and marriage. At times, the decisions of the judicial branch changed, altering the nation forever. With such important issues to decide, the Constitution's protections are essential to the judicial branch. Judges can consider cases with independence and with the security that they won't be punished for their decisions.

The separation of powers helps balance the role of the federal courts with the roles of the other branches of the government. The U.S. Constitution will continue to empower and limit all three branches into the future.

A CLOSER LOOK

THURGOOD MARSHALL WAS A LAWYER WHO SUCCESSFULLY ARGUED IN FRONT OF THE SUPREME COURT IN THE FAMOUS *BROWN V. BOARD OF EDUCATION OF TOPEKA* CASE. HE BECAME THE FIRST BLACK SUPREME COURT JUSTICE.

CHANGING INTERPRETATIONS

The Constitution changes only with an amendment. However, the Supreme Court's understanding of the Constitution has changed over time. Justices bring their own ideas and interpretations of the meaning and intent of the highest law. The Supreme Court's 1896 *Plessy v. Ferguson* decision allowed **segregation** as long as facilities for races were equal. The 1954 *Brown v. Board of Education* decision said that, in education, things that are separate cannot be considered equal. Therefore, segregation in public schools was unconstitutional.

THE WORDS OVER THE ENTRANCE TO THE SUPREME COURT BUILDING REFLECT THE COURT'S GOALS AND RESPONSIBILITIES TO THE AMERICAN PEOPLE.

GLOSSARY

appeal: a legal process by which a case decided in a lower court is brought to a higher court for a new decision

controversy: something that causes arguments

duel: a fight between two people that includes weapons and often happens while other people watch

executive order: an order that comes from the U.S. president or a government agency that must be followed like a law

flexibility: having the ability to do things differently

immigration: the process of coming to a country to settle there

judicial: having to do with courts of law and judges

jurisdiction: the authority to enforce laws

lawsuit: a process by which a court of law makes a decision that ends a disagreement between people or groups

referee: an official who makes sure players follow the rules

segregation: the forced separation of races or classes

testimony: evidence that a witness gives in court

violate: to ignore someone's rights

FOR MORE INFORMATION

BOOKS

Lüsted, Marcia Amidon. *The U.S. Constitution*. Mankato, MN: Child's World, 2016.

MacCarald, Clara. *Establishing the Judicial Branch.* Lake Elmo, MN: Focus Readers, 2017.

Smith-Llera, Danielle. *Exploring the Judicial Branch.* Minneapolis, MN: Lerner Publications, 2019.

WEBSITES

Ben's Guide to the U.S. Government
bensguide.gpo.gov/learning-adventures-4-8
Learn more about the judicial branch and about the other branches of the U.S. government.

Our Constitution: Article III
www.annenbergclassroom.org/resource/our-constitution/constitution-article-iii/
Read about the words and meaning of Article III of the U.S. Constitution.

Publisher's note to educators and parents: Our editors have carefully reviewed these websites to ensure that they are suitable for students. Many websites change frequently, however, and we cannot guarantee that a site's future contents will continue to meet our high standards of quality and educational value. Be advised that students should be closely supervised whenever they access the internet.

INDEX